CW00400850

The Pocketbook of
Porcelain and Pottery Marks

Made of Honour
Antiques
Proprietor: Eric Jones, B.A.

11 City Walls, Chester CH1 1LD (Next to the Eastgate Clock, Wall Level)
☎ (0244) 314208

General Antiques, Books, British Pottery & Porcelain, Staffordshire Figures

MON TO SAT, 10 a.m.–5 p.m.

Est. 1979

LOTS ROAD CHELSEA AUCTION GALLERIES
71 Lots Road (off Kings Road, Chelsea) LONDON SW10 0RN
Open Monday–Saturday
Telephone: 01 352 2349 (24 hrs) and 01-351 5784
AUCTION EVERY MONDAY EVENING AT 6.30 p.m. of
Oriental carpets and textiles (40 lots); paintings and prints
(60 lots); ceramics, glass, silver etc. (100 lots); antique, traditional
and modern furniture (150 lots).
VIEW: Fridays 9–4; Saturdays 10–2; Mondays 9–6.
We can work for you! Quality items always accepted. Payment in 3 days of Sale.

VENNERS ANTIQUES
Mrs S. Davis

7 NEW CAVENDISH ST, LONDON W1
(also at Littlewick Green, Maidenhead, Berks)

Telephone: 01-935 0184

Tues–Fri 10.15–4.30; Sat 10–1

18TH AND 19TH CENTURY PORCELAIN

The Pocketbook of Porcelain and Pottery Marks

Peter Darty

DALTON WATSON LTD.
LONDON

Process Engraving by Star Illustration Works Ltd.
Printed in England by The Lavenham Press Ltd
at Lavenham Suffolk
for the publishers
DALTON WATSON LTD
21 Brook Mews North, London W2
SBN 901564 036

Preface

The story of pottery and porcelain is a fascinating subject.

One learns so much about the styles, techniques and peculiarities of the various factories and potters.

The Tin Glazed Earthenware of the 17th Century, shows how the potter tried to simulate oriental porcelain, whereas the porcelain of the 18th Century depicts the essence of style and taste, which never fails to charm us to-day, and of course is really the most sort after. It is a product of the ultimate in civilised society when time and money were no object.

As a collector myself, I have felt that a pocket book of Marks would be a useful companion to Student and Collector alike.

There are many books on the subject but they are usually large and bulky and not very portable.

In this book I have not shown every Mark there is. What I have tried to do is give an overall picture of some of the more famous ones and a few of the more unusual ones.

P.D.

Acknowledgment

I would like to thank the Factories of Royal Worcester, Royal Doulton, Spode, Copenhagen, for the assistance that they have given. Also my thanks go to Miss Berthalina Large for her help in sorting out my notes and re-drawing some of the Marks I had collected. And Miss Carolyn Russell for typing my notes.

 Jane Pollock Antiques

Proprietors: Jane Pollock

4 Castlegate, Penrith, Cumbria. Tel: 076867211

NINETEENTH CENTURY POTTERY & PORCELAIN

Closed Wednesday, Open Other Days 9.30–5.00

Contents

GLENVILLE ANTIQUES

Proprietor: Mrs. S. E. M. Burgan

120 HIGH STREET, YATTON, AVON BS19 4DH
Tel: 0934 832284

General, mainly 19th Century pottery, porcelain, glass,
sewing items, small furniture.

Monday–Saturday inclusive 10.30 a.m.–1 p.m.; 2.15–5 p.m.

HOPE AND GLORY

Ernest L. Titmuss

131A Kensington Church St, London W8 4BH
Tel: 01-727 8424

TUES–FRI 10–5 p.m.   SAT 10–2.30 p.m.

*Royal Commemorative China and Glass of the
19th & 20th Centuries*

L P J MITCHELL ANTIQUES

27 Camden Passage, Islington, London N1.
Tel: 01-359 7579

GENERAL PORCELAIN
Oriental, English and European Porcelain, Especially
Exports Wares and Ironstone. Some Furniture

TUESDAY – SATURDAY 10 a.m.–4.30 p.m.

Belinda Coote Antiques

29 HOLLAND STREET, LONDON W8 4NA
TEL: 01-937 3924

Mainly 19th Century Pottery & Porcelain.
Specialist in Masons Ironstone China

MON–FRI 10–6   SAT 10–1

Foreword

In every age there have been collectors of beautiful things and there have been people who have wanted to know what things are, who made them and when. Since Chaffers first published his "Marks and Monograms on Pottery and Porcelain" in 1863, there have been many reprints, as well as rival books. Virtually all these have been large volumes more suitable for library shelves than the pocket or briefcase. In more than twenty years no pocket book of marks has been published, and as a result I especially welcome this book. It includes all the important marks used to identify pottery from the earliest times they were used, up to the present century.

It must be borne in mind that marks of the period are only a guide, and a thorough knowledge of the styles and the composition of the paste can be the sole criterion on which to judge the origin of a piece of china. The Meissen crossed swords, the Sèvres interlaced L's, the crowned N of Naples, and the anchor of Chelsea are the marks most often copied. Many of these copies are now well over a hundred years old, and have been handed down through several generations as the genuine thing. There are also the factories which put similar marks to Meissen on their wares, and crossed sticks, scissors, flambeaux, etc., are not Meissen marks. On the other hand it is rare to find a copy of the obscure mark of a little known factory. However, a number of these small concerns produced nearly identical marks, and in some cases it would be unwise to give a definite attribution from the mark alone. One must also beware of ceramics bearing the marks of factories which have become very much more fashionable and valuable than their contemporaries. For example Swansea and Nantgarw marks have been added to genuine English porcelain of the right period.

This book will be useful for all auctioneers and dealers who travel round the countryside, as well as for the amateur, the collector and the person who has old china in his house about which he wants to learn.

Anthony du Boulay

1

2

3

4

5

6

7

8

g.n giuliano Mellone 1541

A f

9

10

P

MAJOLICA EARTHENWARE
ITALY

TUSCANY

Majolica made here in the 16th century.
The typical mark is a capital 'P' of which the
upward stroke forms a loop turned into an 'S'.

Caffaggiolo

- **(1)** 1510
- **(2)** 1540
- **(3)** 1515
- **(4)** Monogram with or without Trident
- **(5)** 1510
- **(6)** 1515
- **(7)** 1515
- **(8)** 1545
- **(9)** 1540
- **(10)** 1515

11

fatatsiena
dann benede
tto

12

IP

13

F (I)

14

DON STORSTO
1489

15

16

Matr° Gio°

17

15 25

M
S

18

15 4 3

GIE

19

MAJOLICA EARTHENWARE — ITALY

SIENA—Tuscany

Pottery made here in the 13th century, Majolica in the 14th and 15th centuries. Revived in the 18th century.

(11)   Siena 1510-20

(12)   Siena, probably Maestro Benedetto

(13)   Maestro Benedetto

URBINO

GUBBIO, Majolica also Lustre wares made here. The famous painter of Lustre, Maestro Giorgio or Giorgio Andrelio worked here and his son Vincezo.

(14)   Mark ascribed to Maestro Giorgio

(15)   Maestro Giorgio

(16)   Maestro Giorgio

(17)   Gubbio Maestro Giorgio with merchant signs or emblems.

(18)   Maestro Giogio

(19)   Gubbio 1519

20

21 CON·POL·DI·S·CASA

22

23

da Urbino

24

25

26

27

28

CASTEL DURANTE, Urbino

Majolica made here in the 16th century. The factory continued until the 18th century.

(20)   Castel Durantė

(21)   Castel Durante

(22)   Possibly one of the Fontana family, a family of Majolica potters who worked at Castel Durante. They were originally called Pellipario. Nicola Pellipario worked at Castel Durante c. 1515-27. Orazio Fontana, grandson of Nicol worked about c. 1565-71.

(23)   Nicola da Urbino

(24)   Nicola da Urbino 1521

(25)   Orazio Fontana

(26)   Orazio Fontana

(27)   Orazio Fontana

(28)   Orazio Fontana

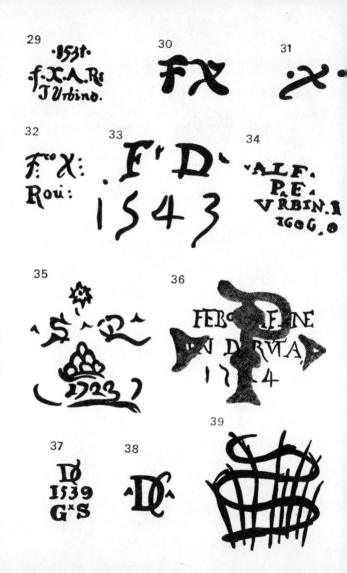

MAJOLICA EARTHENWARE — ITALY

(29)   Francesco Xanto

(30)   Francesco Xanto

(31)   Francesco Xanto

(32)   Francesco Xanto Avelli de Roviga fl 1530-42 was Majolice painter.

(33)   Francesco Durantino

(34)   Alfonso Patanazzi plus Vincenzio and Francesco

SAN QUIRICO d'ORCIA

Majolica was made here from late 17th century to about 1724

(35)   Arms of the Chigi Family

DERUTA, Umbria

Majolica made here before 1500 and during the 17th century.

(36)   Deruta

(37)   Deruta

(38)   Deruta

(39)   Fabriano

MAJOLICA EARTHENWARE — ITALY

ROME

Majolica made at Rome from the 14th century to the 17th century. Porcelain made second half of 18th century.

- **(40)** Rome
- **(41)** Rome, G. Volpatto Roma impressed in the clay.

FAENZA

Centre of Majolica making from the 16th century. Typical marks of the Casa Pirota. Mark of the fire wheel used by leading Majolica makers in Faenza Casa Pirota, worked by Pirotti family.

- **(42)** Faenza
- **(43)** Faenza
- **(44)** Faenza
- **(45)** Faenza
- **(46)** Casa Pirota
- **(47)** Casa Pirota
- **(48)** Casa Pirota
- **(49)** Faenza 1510-1515
- **(50)** 1520
- **(51)** Faenza
- **(52)** Casa Pirota

53 *Marimín:*

54 NOEX

55

56

57

58

59

60

61 *Antonia Terisi in Bassanu*

62 Bº Terchj
Bassano.

63 1564
†

MAJOLICA EARTHENWARE — ITALY

RAVENNA

Majolica made here during the 16th century.

- **(53)** Rimini. All dated from 1535 and 1635.
- **(54)** Rimini. All dated from 1535 and 1635.

VENICE

Majolica made here 1570 until the 18th century.

- **(55)** Venice.
- **(56)** The Bertolini Bros and the Manardi Bros in the 18th century.
- **(57)** Early 18th century Bertolini
- **(58)** Cornaro
- **(59)** Treviso
- **(60)** Bassano possible mark of Terchi who worked at San Quirico d'Orcia, Tuscany 1714-1724, at Siena 1727 and at Bassano 1744.
- **(61)** Terchi
- **(62)** Terchi

PADUA

- **(63)** *Majolica made from end of 15th century to end of 18th century.*

64

65

66

67

68

69

70

71

72 *Milano*
F $\frac{4}{\Omega}$ C

73 *Milano* F·&·C

74

SAVONA

Majolica was made at Savona and Albissola near Genoa in the 16th century to the 18th century. Many marks of workshops recorded.

- **(64)** Lighthouse Pharos of Genoa mark of Levantino
- **(65)** Fishmark of Pescetto
- **(66)** City Arms
- **(67)** Savona same shield with cypher
- **(68)** Solomons Knot mark of Agostino Ratti

TURIN

Majolica made here from the 16th century to the 19th century.

- **(69)** Escutcheon in blue of Charles Emanuel. 1638
- **(70)** Escutcheon of Victor Amadeus. King 1713

MILAN

Majolica was made here in the 18th century.
Potter: Cesare Confalonerie 1775-82 in an oriental style.
FC for Felice Clerice 1745-80

- **(71)** Milan
- **(72)** Milan
- **(73)** Milan
- **(74)** Milan

75

M
Lodi 1764

76

Lodi
M.

77

ue
No:~
G·B·A·B:

78

S.I.G
1750

79

CFC

80

G.G.
pesaro

81

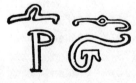

LODI

Majolica made here from 1725. Potter of note Simpliciano Feretti

- **(75)** Lodi
- **(76)** Lodi

LE NOVE near Basano

Founded by B. G. Antonibon. c1762-1835. Made porcelain.

- **(77)** Le Nove
- **(78)** Le Nove

SIENA

Pottery made from 13th century.
Majolica made 14th and 15th centuries to c1520.
Revived 18th century.

- **(79)** Perhaps the initials of Campani, a Majolica Painter who worked at Siena

PESARO near Urbino

Majolica made here in the late 15th and 16th centuries and was revived in the 18th century.

- **(80)** Mark of Casali and Caligari
- **(81)** Pesaro Gabice possibly his mark.

82

83

84

85

86

87

88

89

MAJOLICA EARTHENWARE — ITALY

NAPLES

Majolica made here from the end of the 17th century at the factory of Biagio Giustiniani late 18th century.

- **(82)**   Mark of Biagio Giustiniani
- **(83)**   Mark of Biagio Giustiniani
- **(84)**   Mark of Biagio Giustiniani
- **(85)**   Mark of Biagio Giustiniani
- **(86)**   Mark of Biagio Giustiniani

CAPO DI MONTE

Established by Charles III

- **(87)**   Ferdinado de Vecchio impressed on wares of an Etruscan style.

CASTELLI, Abruzzi

Majolica made from 16th to 18th centuries by the Grue and Gentilli Families.

- **(88)**   Late 18th century
- **(89)**   Liboriuos Grue   d. 1776

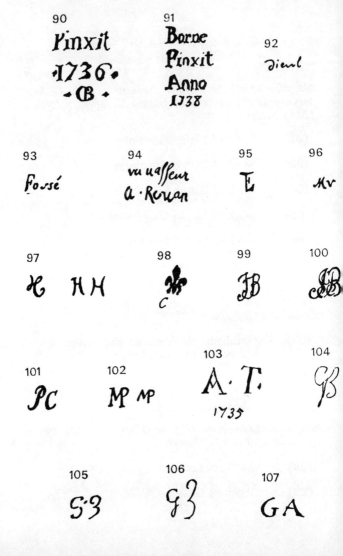

EARTHENWARE

FRANCE

ROUEN

Faïence made here c. 1535-70 and from 1647. Items from 1647 onwards.

- **(90)** Claude Borne
- **(91)** Claude Borne
- **(92)** Dieul, painter c. 1755
- **(93)** Fossé, c. 1740
- **(94)** Levavasseur
- **(95)** Letellier, c. 1780
- **(96)** M. Vallet, 1756
- **(97)** Heugue
- **(98)** Heugue
- **(99)** J. Bertin
- **(100)** J. Bertin
- **(101)** P. Caussy
- **(102)** P. Mouchard, c. 1750
- **(103)** Masseot Abaquesne
- **(104)** Guillibaud factory
- **(105)** Guillibaud factory
- **(106)** Guillibaud factory
- **(107)** Guillibaud factory

108

109

110

Lille

111

112

D2

113

$$\frac{D}{14}$$

114

lille

115

D

116

117

118

119

120

121

122

123

124

LILLE

Faïence made here from 1696 to 1802. A tile works ran until 1808.

(108)	Jacques Febvrier
(109)	Jacques Febvrier
(110)	Jacques Febvrier
(111)	Lille
(112/3)	Bartholomew Dorez

Founded another manufactory when Lille was in the hands of the Dutch 1709-15. His grandson signed N a Dorez.

(114)	Possibly Dorez period

VALENCIENNES

Factory formed 1735 for Hard Paste.

(115)	Fauguez

St. AMAND les EAUX, Nord

Earthenware made in 18th century

(116)	Fauquez
(117)	Fauquez
(118)	Fauquez
(119)	Fauquez
(120)	Fauquez

ILLE DE FRANCE

(121)	Cypher adopted by Claude Revrend 1664
(122)	Cypher adopted by Claude Revrend 1664
(123)	Possible reverse marks
(124)	Possible reverse marks

125

126

127

SCEAUX.

128

129

B. R.

130

131

SÈVRES

132

·S·

133

·S· pellevt

134

·S·c·y·

135

J·R

136

Pj

137

138

R·v·

139

LR

140

Rt

141

M.

142

N

143

SCEAUX (Seine)

Faïence Factory here in 1735 to 1793. by Chappelle let to Julian and Jacques, sold to Glot.

(125)	The S.P. and Anchor marks indicate patronage of the Duke d'Penthièvre.
(126)	S.P. for Sceaux-Penthievre
(127)	Mark at the beginning of Revolution
(128)	Painted mark
(129)	**BOURG la REINE**

Porcelain and Faïence made here by Jullien and Jacques 1774-1814.

ST. CLOUD, Seine-et-Oise.

Faïence made here from 1670.

(130)	Mark of Trout.
(131)	**SINCENY, Aisne.**

Faïence Factory formed here in 1773 onwards, by Jean Baptiste de Fayard.

(132)	Usual Factory mark.
(133)	Mark of Pellevé Manager 1773.
(134)	A rare signature.

APREY, Haute-Marne.

Faïence Factory 1740 to c1860. Factory mark AP accompanied by that of Jacques Jarry and other artists

(135 to 140)	Aprey
(141)	**MATHAUT, Aube.**

Established 18th century.

(142)	**NIDERVILLER, Lorraine**

Faïence made here from 1754 onwards by Beryerlé. Count de Custine 1771. Factory re-opened by Lanfrey 1827 then M. L. G. Dryander.

(143)	Lorraine

144 145 146

147 148 149

150 151 152

 153 154 155

 156 157 158

(144)   Count Custine initials.
(145)   Count Custine initials.
(146)   Count Custine initials.

(147)   SARREGUEMINES, Lorraine.
Faïence factory established here in 1770 by M. Fabry and Paul Utscheider. Made imitation Wedgwood in the 19th century.

(148)   STRASBOURG, Alsace
Faïence made here in the 18th century by the Hannong Family. Hannong Mark.
(149)   Strasbourg.
(150)   Strasbourg.
(151)   Strasbourg.
(152)   Strasbourg.
(153)   Strasbourg.
(154)   Strasbourg.

(155)   PREMIÈRES, Côte D'Or
Faïence factory established here in 1783 near to Dijon by J. Lavelle and carried on until the 19th century.

(156)   MEILLONAS, Bourg en Bresse, Ain
Faïence from 1761-c.1804

(157)   VARAGES, Var, Provence
Freely drawn, factory dated from 1730
(158)   Varages

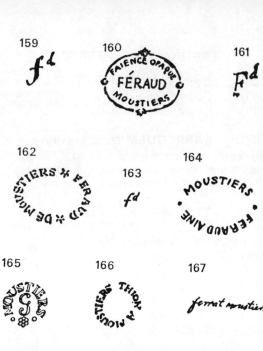

MOUSTIERS, Basses Alpes

Faïence made here in 1679 by Jean-Gaspard Feraud and others until 19th century.

(159)	Jean-Gaspard Féraud 1779-1817
(160)	Jean-Gaspard Féraud 1779-1817
(161)	Jean-Gaspard Féraud 1779-1817
(162)	Jean-Gaspard Féraud 1779-1817
(163)	Jean-Gaspard Féraud 1779-1817
(164)	Jean-Gaspard Féraud 1779-1817
(165)	Joseph-Gaspard Guichard c.1755
(166)	Jean-Francois Thion 1758-1788
(167)	Jean-Baptiste Ferrat 1718-1791

MARSEILLES, Bouches-du-Rhône

Faïence made here from 1677-1827.
Factories of note, Fauchier, Leroy, Perrin, Savy, Robert and Bonnefoy.

(168)	Mark said to be the mark of Savy after the visit of the Comte de Provence in 1777.
(169)	Honoré Savy
(170)	Honoré Savy
(171)	Jaspar Gaspard Robert 1750-95
(172)	Jaspar Gaspard Robert 1750-95
(173)	Jaspar Gaspard Robert 1750-95
(174)	Jaspar Gaspard Robert 1750-95

175   176

V.̇   V͙

177   178

B.   **F.**

179

R

180   181

M   *M*

182   183

fecitte.P.   Rennes
Bourgoin   ce.12.8ᵇʳᵉ
           1763

184

(175)   Veuve Perrin 1748-93

(176)   Veuve Perrin 1748-93

(177)   Antoine Bonnefoy late 18th century.

(178)   Fauchier 1711-95.

(179)   **MARANS, Charente Inférieure**

Faïence made from 1740-1745. Factory transferred to La Rochelle 1756.

(180)   Initial letter of the place.

(181)   Initial letter of the place.

RENNES Ille-et-Vilaine

From 16th century lead glazed earthenware made here, and Faïence from 1748.

(182)   J. B. Alexis Bourgouin modeller
b. 1734

(183)   Rennes.

ORLÉANS, Loiret

Faïence made here from the 17th century

(184)   Gerault Dauraubert

185

J. Boulard a Neuers
1622

186

ILF
1636

187

188

KB
1689

189

H·B
1689

190

E.Borne
II689

193

de conrade
A neuers

191

·F·R·1734

192

N

de Conrade
antuers

194

chollet felit de mouldin 1742

estienne mogdin

NEVERS, Nièvre

Faïence made here after Conrade arrived from Albissola in 1585.

(185)   Early signature.

(186)   Denis Lefebvre

(187)   Jacques Bourdu 1602-1606.

(188)   Henri Borne

(189)   Henri Borne

(190)   Etienne Borne

(191)   Francois Rodriguez

(192)   Nicolas Viodé or Nevers

(193)   Dominique Conrade the Third, 1650-1672.

(194)   **MOULINS, Allier**

Faïence made here in 18th century.

195

*A.+ Limoges +
Le 18me may
J74J*

196

197

*avisseau
atour
1855*

LIMOGES, Haute-Vienne

Faïence factory established here from 1736-1773.

(195)   Mark recorded Limoges and various dates.

AVIGNON, La Tour d'Aigues, (Vaucluse).

Faïence factory founded in 1753.

(196)   Factory mark.

TOURS

Established 1796-1861, reproductions of pottery in the Pallisy and Henri Deux Wares.

(197)   Henri Deux wares signed by Avisseau 1796-1861.

KENDAL STUDIO POTTERY

H. P., A. O. & R. A. Aindow

2/3 Wildman Street, Kendal, Cumbria LA9 6EN.
Tel: 0539-23291

MON–FRI 10.30–1; 3–6. SAT 10.30–1; 3–5

Modern studio pottery made on the premises, also dealers in antiques and works of art.

198

199

200

201

$$\overline{\dfrac{G\,C\,C}{c.\,r,}}$$

202

·IM

203

HP

204

B

205

B. L

206

207

208

M
o
9

209

210

211

IDM

EARTHENWARE
BELGIUM, LUXEMBOURG, HOLLAND

(198)   TOURNAY, Belgium
Established 1750, absorbed by Boch Bros.

(199)   Tournay

(200)   Tournay

(201)   TERVAEREN near Brussels
Established 1720.

(202)   MALINES
Established late 18th century.

(203)   BRUGES

(204)   SEPTFONTAINES, Luxembourg
Septfontaines, the Bros Boch made earthenware here in 1766. In 1841 the factory became one of the Villeroy and Boch Company factories.

(205)   Luxembourg

(206)   Luxembourg

(207)   Luxembourg

DELFT, Holland

(208)   DE METALE POT—The Metal Pot. *Established 1638.* Mark of Pieter Paree 1759-64.

(209 to   DE PAAUW—The Peacock. *Founded*
**211)   1651, closed down 1779.*

212 213 214

215 216
E S WVDB

217 218 219 220 221
IB DB *130 AK AK

222
IDA

223 224 225
DVDD Roos D

226

(212)   Mark deposited by Cornelius Keysor

(213 to   DE TWEE SCHEEPJES—The Two
215)   Little Ships. Mark of Adrian Pynacker
mid 17th to 18th century

(216)   **'T FORTUYN**—The Fortune.
Factory working from 1661-1770
P. Van den Briel mark shown is of Widow Van
den Briel 1764

(217 to   DE WITTE STARRE—The White Star.
221)   *Established 1663 until early 19th*
century. Marks shown Albertus Kiell
1763-72

(222)   **DE VERGULDE BOOT**—The Gold
Boot. *Factory working from 1613 to*
1763. Mark Johhanes den Appel
working 1759.

(223 to   DE ROOS—The Rose. *Factory working*
225)   *from 1666 until mid-19th century. Dirk*
Van der Roos proprietor until 1760

(226)   **DE PORSELEYNE KLAEUW** — The
Porcelain Claw. *Factory working from*
1662 to 1850. Claw marks used
freely with the initials of owners.

227

228
WD

229
$$\frac{ITD}{12}$$

230
DEX
"

231
Z:DEX.
$$\frac{18}{2}$$

232
I H D

233
Hooren

234
M

235
VC

236
E. B. S.

237
GVS

238
GVS

239
RS

EARTHENWARE — BELGIUM & HOLLAND

(227/8) DE DRIE KLOKKEN—The Three Bells. *Working from 1672 to 1840. W D for Van der Goes who registered in 18th century.*

(229 to 232) DE GRIEKSCHE—The Greek. *Factory making pottery in 1658. Adriaenus Kocks 1687-1701*

J. T. DESTRA 1759-65 *then passed to Jacobus Halder Adriaensz. Closed in 1820.*

DE DRIE VERGULDE ASTRONNEN— Three Golden Ash Barrels.

(233) Various owners H Van Hoorn Mark.

(234/5) DE ROMEIN—The Rummer. *Various owners 1613 to about 1769. Signature of Petrus Van Marum 1756-64. Johhanes Vander Kloot 1764-69.*

(236) 'T JONGUE MORIAENSHOOFT 1654 —The Young Moors Head

(237/8) 'T OUDE MORIAENSHOOFT—The Old Moors Head. *Factory working from mid 17th to late 18th century.*

(239) Mark of Rochus Hoppestein 1697.

240 241 242

243 244

245 246

THART thart

247 248

puijn

249 250

De Blompot

EARTHENWARE — BELGIUM & HOLLAND

(240/1) DE PORSELEYNE BIJL—The Porcelain Hatchet.
From the mid-17th century until late 19th century, 1876. Hugo Brouwer owner 1716-1807.

(242/3) DE DRIE PORSELEYNE FLESSIES— The Three Porcelain Bottles. *Various owners from about 1769. Hugo Brouwer marks registered in 1764.*

(244 to 246) 'T HART—The Hart. *Founded 1611 until the late 18th century.*

(247 to 249) DE PORSELEYNE SCHOTEL — The Porcelain Dish. *Factory working in the 17th century 1612, until the late 18th century. Mark of Johannes Van Duyn 1764-1777. Other noted owners, Johannes Pennis 1702-88*

(250) DE VERGULDE BLOMPOT — The Golden Flowerpot. *Working from the early 17th century until 1740's.*

251

D

252

D. S. K.

253

ℓℓ Kan

254

Lℓk

255

⟨ℓℓ⟩

256

W. V. B.

W.13 ANTIQUES

10 THE AVENUE, EALING, LONDON W13 3PH
TEL: 01-998 0390

All Types of Porcelain and Pottery
Good Stock of All Types of Antiques and Collectables

TUES, THURS, FRI, SAT 10–5.30

EARTHENWARE — BELGIUM & HOLLAND

(251)   DE PORSELEYNE FLES—The Porcelain Bottle. *Factory working from 1665 until late 19th century.*

(252)   DE DUBBELE SCHENKKAN — The Double Jug. *Factory founded late 17th century. Famous potter Louwys Fictoor 1689-1714. Mark shown registered in 1764.*

(253 to 255)   DE LAMPETKAN—The Ewer. *Factory founded in early 17th century, 1609 until early 19th century. Mark L P K.*

DE TWEE WILDEMANNEN—The Two Wild Men.

(256)   Willem van Beck after 1760-1778.

Vinci Antiques

Proprietor: Armando Vinci

Jewellery, Silver, Objects of Vertu, Porcelain, Glass-Minature, Watches, Oriental

5 DAYS FROM 10 a.m. to 6 p.m.

124 New Bond Street, London W1. Tel: 01-499 1041

257

B/Z

258

Z

259

Matthias
Rosa
im. Anspach

260

B.B.

261

BK/C

262

B P

263

BP   B.P   BP

264

M

265

A
F.

266

*
H

267

göggingen.
H S

EARTHENWARE

SWITZERLAND, GERMANY, SWEDEN, SPAIN, PORTUGAL

ZURICH

Faïence made here in 1763 and lead glazed earthenware from 1790 to the end of the 19th century.

(257/8)   Zurich. In Blue.

(259)   ANSBACH, Bavaria.

Earthenware made 1710 onwards.

(260/1)   BAYREUTH, Bavaria

Faïence Factory founded 1713 by J. G. Knöller.
Mark in blue—BK for Bayreuth Knöller.

(262/3)   BP for Bayreuth Pfeiffer 1760-67.

(264)   FRANKENTAL, Palatinate. 1755

(265/6)   1800

(267)   GOGGINGEN

268

269

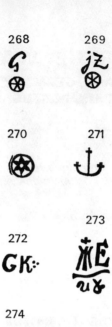

270

271

272

273

274

275

(268) HÖCHST near Mayence.

Faïence made here from 1750 to 1758.

(269/70) Höchst.

Four or six spoke wheels used as marks with painted figures.

(271) POPPLESDORF

Earthenware made here from 1755.

(272) NUREMBURG

Faïence made here from 16th century.

(273 to STRALSUND, Pomerania.
275)

Faïence made here from 1755 by J.U. Giese 1755. Closed in 1790. Arms of the city and the date.

48

276

277

278

M

279

MB

280

281

Künersberg.

282

K
B
L

283

284

(276)   KUNERSBERG, 1754-1768

Faïence factory formed here in 1763 by Tannich succeeded by J. Buchwald, closed in 1788.

(277/8)   KEIL, Holstein.

(279/80) RÖRSTRAND, Sweden.

Faïence Factory founded in 1726, was transferred to Gothenburg in 1926 then to Lidkoping, continues today.

(281/4)   MARIEBERG, near Stockholm.

Faïence and Porcelain made here from 1758 to 1788.

285

Hätt dir
B. dir
Chxit

286

WW
MB:B
X

BL

287

CO>

288

Ać

289

F₂R,

290

B ℳ

EARTHENWARE—SWEDEN, SPAIN, PORTUGAL

(285/6)   MARIEBERG, near Stockholm.

Faïence made here from 1758 to 1788.

(287/8)   ALCORA, Valencia.

Faïence made here from 1726 to 1780. The cream coloured earthenware 1780.

(289/90) LISBON.
Royal Manufactory at RATO.

Faïence made here from 1767.

Helen Buxton Antiques

Proprietor: Helen Buxton

193 Westbourne Grove, London W11 2SB.
Tel: 01-229 9997

*Quality Chinese & Japanese 17th–19th Century Decorative
and Period Porcelain, Furniture & Works of Art*

MONDAY TO FRIDAY 10.00 a.m.–6.00 p.m.

291

292

293

294

295

296   297   298   299

PORCELAIN SOFT-PASTE
ITALY, FRANCE, SPAIN, BELGIUM, SWEDEN

FLORENCE

Porcelain soft paste made from 1575-1581.

(291) Arms of the Medici, with the initials Franciscus Medici Magnus Etruriae Dux Secundus. On pieces for his personal use.

(292) On pieces sent as presents.

(293) Castellani C.

ST CLOUD, Seine-et-Oise

Soft paste made here from 1693. Factory closed in 1766 by the Chicanneau Families.

(294) The Sun in Splendour used 1702-25 denoting the patronage of Louis XIV.

(295) Incised in the paste or painted in blue.

(296) St. Cloud.

LILLE

Soft paste made here from 1711 until 1784. Hard paste made from 1784 to 1790. Closed 1817.

(297) Lille

(298) Lille

(299) Lille

300 301

302 303

·D·V·   **·D·V·**

304 305

306   307   308

S·X   **SP**

309   310   311

          BR

PORCELAIN SOFT-PASTE—FRANCE

CHANTILLY-Oise

Soft paste made from 1725 until 1800.

(300) Mark of a Hunting Horn first painted in red, later rapidly sketched in blue with letters of the decorators sometimes graved in the paste.

(301) Chantilly, in blue.

(302) **MENNECY Seine-et-Oise**

Porcelain made here from 1734 to 1748, then at Bourg la Reine 1833 to 1806

(303) **VINCENNES**
Before 1753.

(304) Letter A between a double L denotes 1753.

(305) B. 1754.

SCEAUX

Porcelain made at Sceaux 1735-93

(306) Almost always graved in the paste

(307) Sceaux

ORLÉANS, Loiret.

Soft paste made here from 1753. Hard paste after 1770.

(308) Orléans

ETOILLES, Seine et Oise

Hard paste porcelain made here from 1768 to 1780.

(309) Jean Baptiste Monier and D Pellevé.

(310) **LA TOUR D'AIGUES, Vaucluse**
1753

(311) **BOURG LA REINE**

Faïence and porcelain made here from 1774 to 1806. by Jullien and Jacques.

312

AR
L

313

A R
L

314

315

316

317

318

MB

319

.M.

320

321

322

323

324

325

326

NOUE

PORCELAIN SOFT-PASTE—FRANCE, BELGIUM, SWEDEN, ITALY

ARRAS, Pas de Calais

Soft paste made here from 1770-86.

(312/3)   A R in blue, purple, crimson.

(314)   TOURNAY, Belgium

Soft paste porcelain made here from 1751 to 1796 by Péterinck. The owner from 1797 to 1799 was C Péterinck Gerrard. Later the Bettignies Family owned the factory—1800-1850.

(315)   In blue, red, brown or gold 1756-81.

(316/7)   MARIEBERG, Sweden

Faïence and porcelain made from 1758-1788.

(318 to   Marks on M B Faïence others in pink
320)   on Porcelain.

(321)   DOCCIA, Near Florence

Porcelain made from 1735 by the Ginori Family and then by Richard Ginori in the late 19th century.

(322 to   Marks—stars in blue red, incised in
324)   red or gold.

LE NOVE

Porcelain made here 1762-1835.

(325/6)   Usual mark 6 points star. G.B.A. stands for Giovanni Battista Antonibon— founder.

327   328

329   330

331   332   333

334   335   336

337

VENICE

(327/8) Vezzi Factory 1720-27 by F. Vezzi 1651-1740.

(329/30) Vezzi marks in blue, red or gold.

(331 to **COZZI FACTORY**
333) 1764. Closed 1818.

CAPO DI MONTE, Naples

Factory started here in 1743 by Charles, King of Naples. Making soft paste porcelain of a yellowish tone. Charles became King of Spain in 1759, the Capo di Monte factory was moved to Buen Retiro, Madrid in 1769.
Paste of the earlier period at Buen Retiro is rather like that of St. Cloud.
The Porcelain of Buen Retiro is not as scarce as that of Capo di Monte and has rather a Spanish style of Decoration. The main style of the Pieces was Neo Classical. The Factory closed in 1808.
Another Factory was opened at Florida near Madrid until 1850 where Sevres styles were much imitated.
Also yet another factory was opened at Naples in 1771, which continued to 1806.
The moulds were bought by the Doccia Factory.

(334) Capo di Monte

(335) Capo di Monte

(336) Capo di Monte

(337) Capo di Monte

338 339

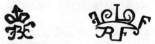

340 341

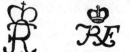

342 343 344

345 346 347

348 349

PORCELAIN SOFT-PASTE—ITALY

(338/9) Capo di Monte

(340/1) Capo di Monte

(342/3) Capo di Monte

(344/5) Capo di Monte

(346/7) Capo di Monte

(348) Capo di Monte

(349) Capo di Monte

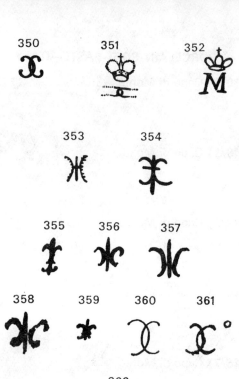

BUEN RETIRO, Madrid

Porcelain made here from 1759 to 1808 after the royal factory transferred from Capo di Monte, Naples. Mark of Bourbon Fleur-de lys used from 1760 to 1804 in various forms.

(350/1) Buen Retiro

(352/3) Buen Retiro

(354/5) Buen Retiro

(356/7) Buen Retiro

(358/9) Buen Retiro

(360/1) Buen Retiro

(362) Buen Retiro

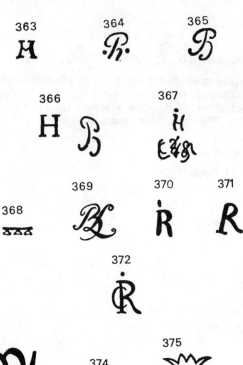

363 364 365
366 367
368 369 370 371
372
373 374 375 376
377 378 379

STRASBURG, Alsace

Faïence was made here in the 18th century, and Porcelain made here by the Hannong Family 1752-1768.

(363 to Marks of the Hannong Family
367) *PH for Paul Hannong 1738.*
J. H. Hannong prop. 1760.

(368) ORLÉANS — a doubtful mark

Factory established here in 1753 for soft paste porcelain. Hard paste from 1770. Factory taken over by Claude Charles Gerault d'Areaubert and came under protection of the Duc de Penthiévre.

(369) Mark stencilled by Benoist Le Brun 1806-1812.

(370/1) MARSEILLES c1770 J. G. Robert dot on the first stroke of the R and P only.

(372) Probably Robert

NIEDERVILLER

A factory for the manufacture of Faïence established 1754. Baron Louis de Beyerlé 1765. Porcelain made from 1765. 1770 factory taken over by Comte de Custine. Factory reopened by Lanfrey and then passed to Dryander in 19th cent.

(373) Beyerle
(374) Custine
(375) Custine
(376) Custine
(377) Custine
(378) Lanfrey
(379) Custine Niederviller

380

381

382

383

384
M.Imp^le
de Sevres.

385

386

387

388

389

390

391

392

PORCELAIN SOFT-PASTE—FRANCE

BORDEAUX

Hard paste porcelain made here from 1781-1787 by Verneuilh and his nephew.

(380)   Verneuilh and nephew

(381)   Bordeaux stencilled Alluaud and Vanier from 1787-1790.

SÉVRES

First at Vincennes 1745 and then moved to Sévres 1756. Then to St. Cloud in 1876. Soft paste porcelain made here from 1745 to 1800. Hard paste from 1769 onwards. The mark is L crossed, issued in many forms at Vincennes, then again at Sévres 1756-1793.

(382)   Year mark 1778

(383)   Republique Française either detached or united with Sévres

(384)   First Empire 1804-14 in red

(385)   Painted in red 1810-14

(386)   In blue 1815-24

(387)   Charles X 1824-29

(388 to 392)   Charles X 1827-30. *Numeral indicates the year*

393

394

395

396

397

398

399

400

401

(393)   Louis Phillipe, in Blue, 1830

(394)   In gold or blue, 1834

(395)   In blue gold 1834

(396)   In chrome green

(397)   In red, second empire 1852-1870

(398)   From 1852

(399)   1872-1879. Mark show year of gilding in red.

(400)   1872-1879. Marks show year of decoration in red.

(401)   1872.

MARKS OR SIGNATURES OF ARTISTS EMPLOYED AT SEVRES FROM 1753

Aloncle
Birds, animals, emblems

André (Jules)
Landscapes

Antreaume
Landscapes and animals

Armand
Birds, flowers, etc.

Asselin
Portraits, miniatures

Aubert ainé
Flowers

Bar
Detached bouquets

𝕭   **Barbin (Francois)**
Ornaments

ℬℬ   **Barrat**
Wreaths, bouquets

ℬ𝒹   **Baudouin**
Ornaments, friezes, or borders

ℬ.𝓇   **Béranger (Antoine)**
Figures

𝟨   **Bertrand**
Detached bouquets

✳   **Bienfait**
Gilding

𝓣.   **Binet**
Detached bouquets

𝒮𝒸.   **Binet (Madame), née Sophie Chanou**
Wreaths, bouquets

𝑃𝑏 **𝒟ℬ** **Boucot**
Flowers, birds, arabesques

        Bouchet
Landscapes, figures, ornaments

Y
Bouillat
Flowers, landscapes

—
Boulanger
Detached bouquets — the same initial, only more slender

ÆB
Boullemier (Antoine)
Gilding

Bn
Bulidon
Detached bouquets

MB m b
Bunel (Madame), née Buteux
Bouquets

9.
Buteux fils, aine
Detached bouquets

△
Buteux fils, jeune
Pastoral subjects, children, etc.

⚓
Buteux père
Flowers, emblems

△
Capelle
Various borders

♀
Cardin
Detached bouquets

5 **Carrier**
Flowers

C **Castel**
Landscapes, hunts, birds

✳ **Caton**
Pastoral subjects, children, portraits

SS **Catrice**
Flowers, detached bouquets

ch **Chabry**
Miniatures, pastoral subjects

cp. **Chapuis ainé**
Flowers, birds, etc.

jc. **Chapuis jeune**
Detached bouquets

JD **Chanou (Madame), born Julie Durosey**
Light borders detached flowers

j.n. **Chavaux fils**
Gilding, detached bouquets

✳ **Chavaux père**
Gilding

Choisy (De)
Flowers, arabesques

Chulot
Emblems, flowers, arabesques

C.m. **Commelin**
Bouquets, wreaths

Cornaille
Detached bouquets, flowers

C. **Couturier**
Gilding

D.i. **Didier**
Ornaments

Dieu
Chinese subjects and flowers, gilding

K. **Dodin**
Figures, subjects, portraits

DR. **Drand**
Chinese subjects, gilding

ADy **Ducluzeau (Madame)**
Figures, subjects

75

𝒟 **Dusolle**
Detached bouquets

DT. **Dutanda**
Bouquets, wreaths

CD. **Duvelly (Charles) (Genre)**
Landscapes and domestic scenes

𝒇 **Evans**
Birds, butterflies, landscapes

F **Falot**
Arabesques, birds, butterflies

𝒥 **Fountain**
Flowers

⸭ **Fontaine**
Emblems, miniatures

♡ **Fontelliau**
Gilding

𝒇x **Fumez**
Flowers, arabesques

𝒢.𝒢. **Georget**
Figures, porttaits, etc.

Gd.   **Gérard**
Pastoral subjects, miniatures

ɤ. t   **Gérard (Madame), née Vautrin**
Bouquets, light borders

ɲ.   **Girard**
Arabesques

Gomery
Birds

Gr.   **Grémont**
Wreaths, bouquets

x.   **Grison**
Gilding

jh   **Henrion**
Wreaths

hc-   **Hericourt**
Wreaths, detached bouquets

Hilken
Figures, pastoral subjects

h.d. **Huard**
Ornaments in various styles

Z. **Joyau**
Detached bouquets

j. **Jubin**
Gilding

D **L. R. La Roche**
Bouquets, wreaths, emblems

L R. **H. La Roche**
Bouquets, wreaths, emblems

L.B. **Le Bel**
Landscapes

L°. **Le Bel ainé**
Figures and flowers

LB. LB **Le Bel jeune**
Wreaths, bouquets

L.G. **Le Guay (Et. Charles)**
Figures, subjects, portraits

LG. *LG.* **Le Guay**
Gilding

LL *LL* **Lecot**
Chinese subjects, etc.

∪ **Ledoux**
Landscapes and birds

Leguay
Miniatures, children

F. **Levé (Félix)**
Flowers, Chinese subjects

L L **Levé Père**
Flowers, birds, arabesques

RB. **Maqueret (Madame), née
Bouillat**
Bouquets

M. **Massy**
Flowers and emblems

S. **Mereaud ainé**
Various borders

9 **Mereaud jeune**
Bouquets, wreaths

X **Micaud**
Flowers, bouquets, clock dials

M:m **Michel**
Detached bouquets

M **Moiron fils**
Detached bouquets

M. **Morin**
Marine and military subjects, Cupids

Å **Mutel**
Landscapes

nq. **Niquet**
Detached bouquets

Noël
Flowers, ornaments

D. **Nouailher (Madame), née Sophie Durosey**
Detached flowers, light borders

P **Parpette**
Flowers

LP **Parpette (Mademoiselle Louison)**
Detached flowers

f. **Pfeiffer**
Detached bouquets

S.h. **Philippine**
Flowers and ornaments

P1 *p.7.* **Pierre jeune**
Bouquets, wreaths

S.k. **Pithou aîné**
Portraits, historical subjects

S.j. **Pithou jeune**
Figures, flowers, ornaments

6 **Pouillot**
Detached bouquets

Æ. **Poupart (Achille)**
Landscapes

HP. **Prévost**
Gilding

Raux
Detached bouquets

 Rocher
Figures

 Rosset
Landscapes, etc.

 Rousselle
Detached bouquets

 Schadre
Birds, landscapes

Sinsson
Flowers, groups, wreaths

S.S.P. **Sinsson (Pierre)**
Flowers

Sioux ainé
Detached bouquets, wreaths

O **Sioux jeune**
Flowers and wreaths in camaton

Swebach
Landscapes and domestic scenes

Taillandier
Bouquets, wreaths

••• Tandart
Groups of flowers, wreaths

⬛ Tard
Detached bouquets

•••• Théodore
Gilding

***jt.* Thevenet fils**

ſ Thevenet père
Flowers, dials, groups

𝒟. Vandé
Gilding, flowers

W. Vavasseur
Arabesques

⬛ Vieillard
Emblems, ornaments

2000 Vincent
Gilding

✠ ✠ Xrouet
Landscapes

CHRONOLOGICAL TABLE

Chronological table of the Marks employed at the Sèvres Manufactory from 1753, to indicate the year in which the piece was decorated.

Year Marks 1753-1777	Year Marks 1778-1793	Date Signs 1801-1817
A (Vincennes) 1753	AA .. 1778	T.9 .. 1801
B (Vincennes) 1754	BB .. 1779	X .. 1802
C (Vincennes) 1755	CC .. 1780	// .. 1803
D .. 1756	DD .. 1781	÷ .. 1804
E .. 1757	EE .. 1782	
F .. 1758	FF .. 1783	-//- .. 1805
G .. 1759	GG 1784	ᴠ .. 1806
H .. 1760	HH .. 1785	
I .. 1761	II .. 1786	7 .. 1807
J .. 1762	JJ .. 1787	8 .. 1808
K .. 1763	KK .. 1788	9 .. 1809
L .. 1764	LL .. 1789	10 .. 1810
M .. 1765	MM .. 1790	oz .. 1811
N .. 1766	NN .. 1791	dz .. 1812
O .. 1767	OO .. 1792	tz .. 1813
P .. 1768	PP .. 1793	qz .. 1814
Q .. 1769		qn .. 1815
R .. 1770		sz .. 1816
S .. 1771		ds .. 1817
T .. 1772		
U .. 1773		
V .. 1774		
X .. 1775		
Y .. 1776		
Z .. 1777		

402   403   404

405   406   407

408   409

C.D

410   411

PORCELAIN HARD-PASTE

GERMANY, HOLLAND, BELGIUM, RUSSIA, POLAND,
AUSTRIA, CZECHSLOVAKIA, HUNGARY, PORTUGAL

FAUBOURG ST. DENIS or FAUBOURG ST. LAZARE — Paris
Hard paste made from 1771 to 1810 (22)
(402)   Initials of Hannong
(403)   Initials of Charles Philippe
(404)   Same under a crown

RUE de LA ROUQUETTE — Paris
White Faïence made 18th century by Ollivier.
(405)   Hard paste from 1773 Soroux's Mark.

LA COURTILLE or Rue Fontaine-au-Roy or Basse Courtille, Faubourg du Temple, Paris
Hard paste made here 1771, closed in 1841.
(406)   Incised
(407)   In blue
(408)   In blue

LIMOGES, Haute-Vienne
(409 to *Hard paste made here from 1783 by*
410)   *Massié and others.*

RUE de REUILLY, Paris
Hard Paste Porcelain made here by Jean-Joseph Lassia from 1774-1778.
(411)   1774-1784 in gold or colour

CLIGNANCOURT, Paris
Factory founded late 18th century under patronage of Monsieur Louis-Stanislas-Xavier, Compte de Provence, the King's brother. In the style of Sévres.

412 413 414

415 416 417

418
P
C G

419

420

421 422 423 424

- **(412)** Blue
- **(413)** In gold
- **(414)** M. for Monsieur
- **(415)** Lsx Stencilled Louis Stanislas Xavier
- **(416)** Same initial
- **(417)** Stencilled in red 1775-1793

(418) RUE du PETIT CAROUSEL, Paris
A decorating Establishment run by Charles-Barthélémy Guy and continued by his son Charles until 1800.

BOISETTE, near Melun, Seine-et-Marne
Porcelain made from 1777 to 1792.
(419 to Blue B. Various forms
420)

RUE THIROUX, Paris
André — Marie Leboeuf. Patron, Marie Antionette, called Porcelain de la Reine. Hard paste Porcelain made here 1775. Her Monogram and a Crown as Mark. After revolution Guy and Housel took over factory 1797-1798 and Leveillé factory closed in 1820.
(421 to Painted. Later stencilled. All in Red.
423)
(424) Guy and Housel, Leboeuf's successors.
The porcelain is later inscribed Leveillé 12 Rue Thiroux.

425

426

427

428

MANUFACTURE DE MONSⁿ
LE DUC D'ANGOULEME
A PARIS

429

DIHL ET
GUERHARD
A PARIS

430

GUERHARD
ET DIHL
A PARIS

431

MANUFACT^{RE}
DE DIHL ET
GUERHARD

432

NAST

433

RUE DE BONDY, Paris

From 1780 by Guerhard. Hard past porcelain from c. 1786, at Rue du Temple 1795, and Boulevard Saint Martin 1825.

(425)　　Early mark Guerhards initial.

(426)　　Initial of Duc d'Angouléme (patron).

(427 to Later marks in Red.
431)

RUE DE POPINCOURT, Paris

Hard paste porcelain made here from 1722 by Nast and continued by his sons in 19th century.

(432)　　Stencilled in Red

LILLE

Soft Paste made here from 1711 to 1730.
Hard paste porcelain made here from 1784 to 1790 by Le perre-Durot then it had various owners. Closed in 1817.

(433)　　Dolphin was adopted because the factory was protected by the Dauphin

434

435

436

B
Potter
42

437

R
C·P
1

438

JP

439

caen

440

CREIL

VALENCIENNES, Nord

Hard paste made here in 1785 assisted by J. B. Fauquez helped by Lamoninary (Brother in Law) 1800-1810.

(434)   Cypher of Fauquez Lamoninary and Valenciennes.

(435)   CHOISY-le-ROY, Seine

Hard paste porcelain made in the late 18th century.

RUE DE CRUSSOL, Paris

Porcelain made here in 1789 by Christopher Potter (English).

(436/7) In Underglaze blue. May have been transferred to E. Blancheron 1792

BELLEVILLE, Fountainbleu

Hard paste made here by Jacob Petit in 1790.

(438)   Mark in blue

(439)   CAEN CALVADOS

Hard paste made c. 1793-1806. Factory of d'Aigmont Desmares and Ducheval.

(440)   CREIL, OISE

Earthenware in the English style made here 1794-1895.

441   442   443

444   445   446

447   448   449

450   451

MEISSEN, near Dresden, Saxony

Red stoneware made early 18th century until c. 1730, under J. F. Bottger (fl.1704-1719). Hard paste porcelain produced here by 1713 but not marked until 1724.

(441) Impressed, incised or moulded

(442) Impressed, incised or moulded

(443) Pseudo-Chinese marks occurred on blue and white porcelain (*c.* 1720-1725) and on stoneware.

(444) Johanneum Inventory No.27

(445/6) Caduceus Mark used *c.* 1723

(447) 1725-1750

(448) 1725

(449) 1763-1774

(450) 1763-1774

(451) 1774-1814

452

K. P. M

453

M P M

454

455

456

457

458

459

460

(452)   First identifiable factory marks

(453)   First identifiable factory marks sometimes with crossed swords

(454)   Variant mark of crossed swords

(455 to 457)   Sub-standard ware was cancelled this way

(458/9)   Augustus Rex cypher. *Placed in blue on fine pieces for the Royal Palace. Forged often, in 19th century.*

(460)   Modern Mark

461

462

463

464

465

466

467

468

469

470

471

472

FÜRSTENBURG, Brunswick
Porcelain made here 1747-1859 and continued.
(461/2) All in blue.
(463) Mostly found on biscuit porcelain

HÖCHST near Mayence
Porcelain made from 1750-1798.
(464) Wheel mark in red or red enamel 1750-1762.
(465) With crown 1765-1774 impressed from 1760-1765, 6 spokes.
(466) Höchst

(467) FULDA, Hesse
Porcelain made here from 1765-1790.
(468/9) Mark FF for 'Fürstlich Fuldaisch' which forms the letter for Heinrich Von Bibra who founded the factory.

GOTHA, Thuringia
Established 1757, continues
(470) After 1880

(471) WALLENDORF, Thuringia
Porcelain made in 18th century by the Hammann & Greiner families. Closed 1833.

(472) ARNSTADT
Established about 1808

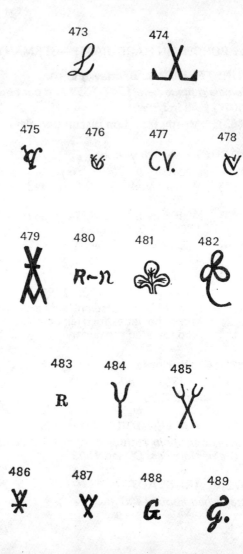

(473/4) LIMBACH, Thuringia

Porcelain factory founded 1772 G. Greiner

KLOSTER VEILSDORF, Thuringia

Hard paste factory established 1760.

(475 to Marks 1760 onwards
478)

(479) ANSBACH, Bavaria

Hard paste 1758-1762. Moved to Castle of Bruckberg 1762-1806. Sold 1806. Continued to 1860.

(480) RAUENSTEIN, Thuringia

Hard paste made by Greiners in 1783. Continues today.

(481/5) GROSZBREITENBACH, Thuringia

Hard paste from late 18th century. From 1869 the firm was Bühl and Söhne.

486/7) VOLKSTEDT, Thuringia

Porcelain factory established at Sitzendorf 1760. Moved to Volkstedt 1762.

(488/9) GERA, Thuringia

Faïence made 1752-1780

490

491

492

493

494

495

496

497

498

BADEN-BADEN

Porcelain factory 1770-1778.

(490/1) Zacharias Pfalzer

LUDWIGSBURG, Württemberg

Hard paste from 1758-1824.

(492) Customary mark

(493) Same with crown I for Duke Ludwig 1793-1795.

(494/5) Painted in blue 1758-1793

(496) King William 1816-1824

(497/8) Stag horns from the arms of Württemberg painted in blue, late 18th or early 19th.

499   500   501

502   503

504 505 506

507 508

NYMPHENBURG, Bavaria

Hard paste porcelain made here 1755 to 1862.

(499) 1763-1777

(500) Factory Marks

(501) Factory Marks

(502 to ANSBACH, Bavaria

504) *Hard paste porcelain made here 1758-1762. Moved to Castle of Bruckberg 1762-1806. Sold 1806, continued to 1860.*

(505) Also with eagle in blue

(506/7) Impressed on figures

BAYREUTH

Porcelain made during the 18th century. J. C. Schmidt founded a factory in early 19th century.

(508) Hard paste, cream coloured earthenware counterfeit mark of Wedgwood used.

509

510 WE

511 W

512

513

K.P.M.

514

515

PROSKAU

516

517

518

519

PORCELAIN HARD-PASTE—GERMANY, CZECHOSLOVAKIA, AUSTRIA, HUNGARY

BERLIN

(509 to 511) Porcelain Factory, marks in blue or impressed Wegely marks

(512) Became a royal establishment, Gotzkowsky's Factory made porcelain from 1761 onwards. From 1763 the Sceptre mark was used. KPM with orb 1830's.

(513) From 1813 Königliche Porzellan.

(514) 1823-1832, 1884-1897.

(515) PROSKAU, Silesia

Faïence made here from 1763 until 1850. Proskau impressed 1788-1850.

VIENNA

Hard paste porcelain factory founded in 1719-1864. Du Paquier assisted by Stölzel. Closed in 1864. Du Paquier period no marks, perhaps a Chinese one.

(516) Shield used 1744 onwards. Year marks 1738-1800.

SCHLAGGENWALD, Bohemia

Hard paste porcelain factory in 1792.

(517) Paulus, Pöschl and Reumann. S. painted or incised.

Factory owned by Lipert Hass from 1803-1843. Continued.

(518) ELBOGEN

Porcelain made 1815 by Springer and Co.

(519) HEREND

Porcelain factory founded 1839 Moritz Fisher specialised in copies of European and Oriental porcelain.

520 521

522 523 524

Amstel

525

526 527 528

529 530

PORCELAIN HARD-PASTE
HOLLAND AND BELGIUM

WEESP 1764-1771

(520)　　In underglaze blue.

(521)　OUDE.　*Transferred from Weesp Porcelain Factory 1771 until 1784. Transferred to Amstel M.O.L. incised.*
Hard paste porcelain from 1759-1771. Transferred to Oude Loosdrecht 1771, then to Amstel 1784.

(522/3) AMSTEL

Hard paste from 1784 to 1820 in blue.

(524/5) THE HAGUE

Hard paste porcelain 1775-1785.

SEPTFONTAINES, Luxemburg

Boch Brothers made earthenware 1766-1796.

(526 to　P. J. Boch, sole proprietor in 1796.
529)

KERAMIS LE LOUVIÈRE, Hainault

Earthenware Factory established 1841.

(530)　　Boch Frères

531 532 533

534

535

536 537 538

539 540 541 542

(531)   ZURICH
Porcelain made here 1763, mark in blue.

NYON, Geneva
Hard paste made from 1781. Jacques Dortu until 1813.
(532)   Fish in blue underglaze.

COPENHAGEN
Royal Copenhagen Porcelain Manufactory from 1775, continues.
(533)   Hard paste. Marks: 3 wavy lines, the emblems of the three Danish Waterways leading into the Baltic. *Adopted in 1775.*

(534)   VISTA ALEGRE
Hard paste porcelain factory started by J. F. P. Basto in 1824. Continues today.

TURIN
Hard paste porcelain between 1737-1742. Rare.
(535)   DG in black, Gionetti

ST. PETERSBURG or Petrograd or Leningrad
Hard paste porcelain made here from 18th century. Factory established under the patronage of Catherine II.
(536)   In blue
(537)   In blue
(538)   Court Inventory Mark — Catherine II 1762-1796
(539)   Paul I, 1796-1801
(540)   Alexander I, 1801-1825
(541)   Nicholas I, 1825-1855
(542)   Alexander II 1855-1881

543

544

545

546

547

ВРАТЬЕВЪ
Корниловыхъ

548

549

С

550

Э

551

А

552

ГАРДНЕРЪ

PORCELAIN HARD-PASTE—RUSSIA

(543) Alexander III 1881-1894

(544) Nicholas II, 1894-1917

(545) Soviet, 1917

(546) Alexander II. *In 1871 a dot was added to the signature, a second dot was added and so on.*

(547) Korniloff Mark. *Factory established 19th century.*

(548) Korniloff

MOSCOW

Factory established here by Gardners 1758 hard paste porcelain.

(549) In blue

(550) In blue

(551) In blue

(552) Impressed

553

ПОПОВЫ

554

АП

555

АР

556

АР

557

Ф Г
ГУАИНА

558

KIEBZ
13
II

559

Korzec

PORCELAIN HARD-PASTE
RUSSIA AND POLAND

POPOFF, Moscow

(553 to 1806-1872
556)

(557/8) KIEF

*Cream coloured earthenware made from end of
18th century.*

(559)   KORZEC, or Koretki

*Hard paste porcelain made 1790. Transferred to
Gorodnitza 1797, closed in 1870.*

SUE NORMAN

Sue & Mick Alloway

L4 ANTIQUARIUS, 135 KINGS ROAD SW3
Tel: 01-352 7217

Blue & White Transferware and Ironstone China, from the
Early 19th Century

Monday–Saturday 10.30–5.30

560

561

562

563

564

565

566

Chelfea 1745

567

568

569

570 571 572 573 574

575 576 577

POTTERY & PORCELAIN
ENGLAND

BOW, c. 1747-1776

Many factory and workmans marks are recorded, but the most generally recognised are after 1760 — an anchor and a dagger in red or underglaze blue.

(560/1) 1750-1755

(562 to 565) The painted anchor and dagger mark was the standard Bow mark from 1760-1776. As this was painted by hand many variations occur and on some rare examples only the dagger was painted The Crescent mark in underglaze blue occurs on some pieces also on figure not to be confused with the Worcester Crescent mark.

CHELSEA

Factory established c. 1745.
Making porcelain until 1784, under different managements. Eventually bought by William Duesbury and John Heath of Derby. The products of the years 1770-1784 are known as Chelsea Derby. Closed down 1784.

Four clearly defined periods:

(566/7) 1 Triangle 1745-1749

(568/9) Raised Anchor 1750-1753

(570/1) Red Anchor 1753-1758

(572 to 577) Gold Anchor 1758-1770

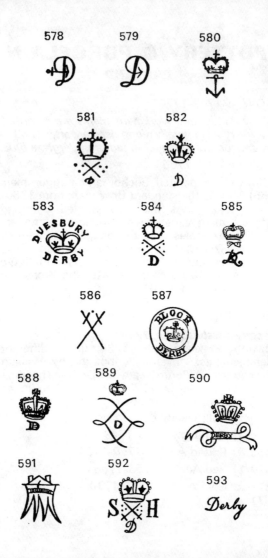

578 579 580

581 582

583 584 585

586 587

588 589 590

591 592 593 Derby

(578 to W. Duesbury was working the **Chelsea**
580) Factory, from 1769-1775.

CHELSEA DERBY

The following marks were used plus an anchor.

(581) Standard Painted Mark 1782-1825

(582) Painted Derby porcelain 1771-1782

(583/4) Adopted by Dusebury 1800 rare
imitations

(585) Very rare mark 1795

(586) Mock Dresden mark 1785-1825

(587) Bloor Mark 1820-1840

(588) Printed Mark in red 1825-1840

(589) Painted Mock Sevres mark 1825-1848

(590) Printed in Red 1830-1848

(591) Painted Chinese type patterns. Variations
occur 1760-1780

(592) 1861-1935

(593) 1750-1755 Rare incised

594 595

596 597

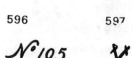

598 599 600 601 602

603 604

605 606 607

DERBY

Porcelain made from 1745 to 1848. Then from 1876 onward. Owned by William Duesbury 1756 then his son William, then Michael Kean. Works bought in 1811 by Robert Bloor. Closed 1848. Royal Crown Derby Porcelain Company founded 1876.

(594) 1750

(595) 1780

(596) 1795

(597) 1830

(598) 1760 Chelsea Derby

(599) 1770-1780 Chelsea Derby

(600) 1784 Chelsea Derby

(601) 1784-1810 Chelsea Derby

(602 to 1795-1796 Imitation
604)

(605 to Imitation
607)

608

609   610

611   612   613

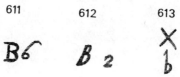

614

615

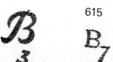

616   617

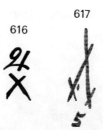

PLYMOUTH & Bristol

William Cooksworthy, 1768-1770, took out a patent for hard paste porcelain.

(608) Mark — the sign for tin or jupiter in underglaze blue or in overglaze enamel. Workman's marks may occur but are not factory marks.

Cooksworthy transferred his manufactory to Bristol in 1770 to Champion Works and sold him the patent. Soft paste made from c. 1749 to 1752 when factory amalgamated with Worcester. Hard paste from 1770 to 1786.

(609/ 610) Bristol Mark usually a cross in blue or impressed, usually accompanied by numbers denoting the different decorators.

(611 to 615) B was a common mark

(616) Plymouth and Bristol marks combined.

(617) Painted marks after 1770-1780. Cross swords in imitation of the Dresden Mark usually painted in blue underglaze.

618

RALPH·OFT.

619

thomas:toft

620

THOMAS TOFT

621

thomas TOFT

622

AAAS

623

624

625

626

627

TURNER

(618) TOFT, Ralph. (b.1638)
On large Toft-style dishes.

(619 to TOFT, Thomas (d.1689). Name occurs on
622) wares decorated with trailed slip, the
dishes having trellis rimborders with the
name.

LIVERPOOL

*Many potters made varied wares in Liverpool
during the 18th century. Most tinglazed Delft type
are unmarked.*
*John Sadler c. 1756-1799 invented a process of
ceramic printing and other potters sent their
wares to be printed by Sadler & Green.*

(623/4) Heculaneum founded 1793. Various
ownerships made earthenware and stoneware porcelain of the Staffordshire type.
174 Liver birds marks in many forms.
173 impressed or printed marks 1796-
1833

(625/6) Longton Hall, Staffordshire, England.
Porcelain factory here c. 1750. Closed
1760. William Littler in partnership with
Aaron Wedgwood, trading as Littler &
Co, 1752-1760.

(627) TURNER & ABBOT, Lane End, Longton,
Staff potteries. Wedgwood type jasper
wares 1785-1787.

628

Absolon yarm ⊕

629

SCOTT
PB

630

LEEDS · POTTERY
LEEDS · POTTERY

631

HARTLEY GREENS & Co
LEEDS POTTERY
HARTLEY GREENS & Co
LEEDS POTTERY

632

HARTLEY · GREENS & Co.
LEEDS · POTTERY

633

634

LEEDS * POTTERY
LEEDS * POTTERY

(628) Absolom William, The Ovens, 25 Market Row, Yarmouth, Norfolk. Decorator of earthenwares 1784-1815.

(629) Portobello, Nr. Edinburgh, Scotland. Scott Bros. Earthenwares c. 1786-1796.

LEEDS, The Old Pottery. c. 1760-1878.

(630 to 634) Established at Hunslet, Leeds 1760 by the two Green brothers, later trading as Hartley, Greens & Co, making cream coloured earthenware 1780-1820 with pierced or basket work. Sold in 1825, then trading as S. Wainwright & Co; the Leeds Pottery Co; and Warburton, Britton & Co.

NEW HALL

(635) Shelton Staffordshire Factory, making hard paste 1782, changing to Bone China from 1810 until its closure in 1835.

PINXTON

Derbyshire Porcelain made here from 1796-1812.

(636/7) Most are unmarked or the name Pinxton written rare.
After William Billingsly left 1799 John Coke continued and rarely used a mark, a star and crescent from his family arms with curvasive letter P with or without a number.

635

New Hall

636

Pinxton
343

637

P
N 300

638

W

639

E

640

X

641

642

ROCKINGHAM

Rockingham Works
Brameld.

643

644

SWANSEA

645

CAMBRIAN

646

NANT-GARW
G.W.

647

Davenport

LOWESTOFT, Suffolk

(638 to Factory making soft paste porcelain here
641) in 1757-1802. No mark consistently used. Factory marks of Worcester, Meissen, and other factories sometimes imitated.

ROCKINGHAM

Earthenwares and porcelain from 1826. Early wares were unmarked.
Brameld took over factory in 1806, many Brameld earthenware marks occur from 1806 to 1842.

(642) The Griffin mark printed at first in red, on some samples the crest occurs without any wording.

SWANSEA, Glamorganshire

(643 to Earthenware was made here 1764-1870
645) and porcelain from 1815-1817. Porcelain incorporation soapstone after 1817-1823 at the Cambrian pottery under different owners, trading as Haynes, Dillwyn & Co. 1802-1810. T. J. Bevington & Co. 1817-1824, and Dillwyn again 1831-1850. Finally David Evans and his son. Marks — Tridents or Cambrian.

NANTGARW, Glamorganshire

(646) Founded 1813-1820 by William Billingsly. Porcelain a fine translucent body. Transferred to Swansea for a while. Billingsly at Nantgarw 1816-1820.

C (((C (C C C c S S S S •

650

TURNER

651

652

653

SALOPIAN

654

655

656

657

658

659

660

661

DAVENPORT, 1793-1882

(647) Various styles. W. Davenport & Co., Davenports Ltd. etc. Longport Staffordshire Potteries.
Earthenwares, creamwares, porcelains, ironstone etc.

CAUGHLY, Shropshire

Porcelain made here from 1772 by Thomas Turner. John Rose of Coalport took over from Factory 1799; it closed down in 1814. Various marks used.

(648) Crescent or C marks in blue underglaze, the filled shade pieces are used on printed wares. 1775-1790.

(649) Printed marks in underglaze blue 1775-1790.

(650) Turner 1775-1780 impressed

(651/2) Printed mock Chinese signs with English numerals printed in underglaze blue.

(653) Salopian in full impressed

(654 to 661) Turners disguised initials

Most examples of Caughly porcelain, decorated with the enamelled decoration, are unmarked.

662 *Coalport*

663 *CDale*

664 *CD*

665

666

667

668

669

670

671 JOHN ROSE & Co / ENGLISH PORCELAIN / COALPORT

672 ROSE & / Coalbrookdale / Porcelain

673 JOHN ROSE & Co. COALBROOKDALE SHROPSHIRE

674

COALPORT of Coalbrookdale, Shropshire. 1796 (at Stoke on Trent from 1926).
By John Rose & Co., making porcelain continued by his descendants until 1862. In 1855 it was owned by a member of the Bruff Family and was sold in 1924 to Cauldon Potteries, Ltd., moving to Staffordshire in 1926.

(662 to The early Coalport was mostly unmarked.
666)

COLEBROOKDALE

(667)   **(668)**   **(669)**   **(670)**

(671)   **(672)**   **(673)**   **(674)**

675 676

677

678 679

680

681 682

MINTON

Minton. Stoke on Trent. Earthenware and Porcelain 1793 onwards. Thomas Minton & Son 1817. Minton Hollins & Co. 1845-1868 Minton & Co. From 1883 as Minton Ltd.

(675)   Transfer printed 1800-36

(676/7) Same

(678)   Printed or Impressed after 1851.

(679/ 680) Printed Marks 1860

(681)   Minton, late 19th/early 20th century.

(682)   Revised standard Mark 1873.

683

684

685

686

687

688

689

690

MINTON

691

MINTONS

692

B B New Stone

(683)   1822-1836

(684)

(685)   Transfer printed 1860-1880

(686)   Transfer printed

(687)   Transfer printed

(688)   Transfer printed M. 1822-1830
             M & Co. 1841-1844
             M & M. 1845-1868

(689)   Transfer printed, uranium glaze, 1918

(690)   Impressed 1861 onward

(691)   Impressed 20th century

(692)   Impressed

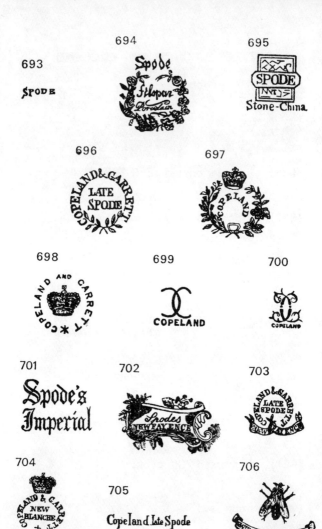

693

SPODE

694

Spode
Felspar
Porcelain

695

SPODE
Stone-China

696

COPELAND & GARRETT
LATE
SPODE

697

COPELAND

698

COPELAND AND GARRETT

699

COPELAND

700

COPELAND

701

Spode's
Imperial

702

Spodes
NEW FAYENCE

703

COPELAND & GARRETT
LATE
SPODE
NEW FAYENCE

704

COPELAND & GARRETT
NEW
BLANCHE
+ L.I.

705

Copeland Late Spode

706

LATE COPELAND & SONS

SPODE

Earthenware factory founded 1770. Porcelain *c.*
1800, by Josiah Spode, Stoke-on-Trent. Called
Spode Copeland 1813. Copeland Garret 1833.
Copeland late Spode 1847. After this Copeland
alone; continues today.

(693)   1800 printed puce or gold

(694)   Spode in blue

(695)   Printed in blue, early 19th century

(696)   1833-1847

(697)   Copeland Garret

(698)   Copeland Garret

(699)   Copeland 1847-1851

(700)   Copeland

(701 to Earthenware
706)

707

↗

♂

ROGERS

708

Opaque China
B and C

710

DOULTON
LAMBETH

712

711

Lambeth Pottery
DOULTON & WATTS
+15+
HIGH STREET
LAMBETH

DOULTON
LAMBETH

713

DOULTON
LAMBETH

DALE HALL, Longport

(707)   Staffordshire potteries. 1784-1814.
Later J. Rogers & Son.

(708)   Hilditch & Son, Church St., Lane End.
Staffordshire potteries 1822-1830. China
and earthenwares.

(709)   Bridgwood & Clarke, Church Yard Works,
Burslem also at Tunstall 1864. 1857-
1864 Edward Clarke & Co. Earthenwares.

DOULTON:1815

710 to 713

John Doulton 1793-1837 became a partner in
Doulton & Watts 1815 at Lambeth, London,
made salt-glazed stoneware; firm traded as
Doulton & Co from 1854 continues. Decorative
stoneware made at Lambeth from 1870, also at
Burselm, Staffordshire 1877. Bone china made
from 1884.

714

715

716

717

718

719

720

W. De Morgan & Co

London 1891

721

POTTERY & PORCELAIN—ENGLAND

(714 to De Morgan, William Frend, 1839-
721) 1917. English potter made reproductions of 16th and 17th century Syrian wares with lustre decoration. Worked London, Merton Abbey, Surrey 1882-1888; in partnership with Halsey Ricardo at Fulham 1888-1889 and again 1898-1907.

ATRIUM ANTIQUES

W. L. & M. G. Richardson

53/55 CHURCH ST, GUISBOROUGH, CLEVELAND
Tel: Guisborough 0287 32777

GENERAL ANTIQUES

Tues, Thurs, Fri & Sat. 10.30–12.30 & 2.30–4.30

LIBRA ANTIQUES

Anna M. Wolsey

**131E Kensington Church Street (Peel Street),
London W8. Tel: 01-727 2990**

Blue & White & Other Early English & European Pottery

MON–FRI 10–5.30, SAT 10–4

722

Mason's Patent
Iron Stone China.

723

724

725

726

727

728

729

730

(722 to 730) Mason Family, fl.1795-1854 Staffordshire potters; Miles Mason 1752 1822, made porcelain at Fenton from 1800, bone china 1807-1813; succeeded by G. M. Mason then C. J. Mason, porcelain, bone china, and ironstone china; C. J. Mason again at Longton 1851, closed in 1854.

ZELLI'S

Proprietor: V. Zelli

62 Burlington Arcade, London W1. Tel: 01-493 0203

Fine porcelain figurines of animals and birds by Meissen, Nymphenburg, Hutschenreuther and other famous manufactors Hand sculptured figurines by a number of English artists

MON–FRI 9–5.30 p.m.   SAT 9–1 p.m.

CLUNES ANTIQUES

Proprietor: Daphne Clunes

9 West Place, Wimbledon Common, London SW19 4UH
Tel: 01-946 1643

Staffordshire Figures, Carpentry Tools, Small Furniture, Theatricalia, Small Objects of Interest

TUES, THURS, FRI, SAT 10–5 p.m.

JOSIAH WEDGWOOD, 1730-1795

English Pottery at Burslem, Staffordshire making all kinds of Wares except Bone China and Porcelain. Partnership with Whieldon 1754-1759. Trading as Wedgwood & Bentley 1769-1780. Factory inherited by Wedgwood's son Josiah; and continues today. **(731 to 748)**

731

732

733

WEDGWOOD

734

JOSIAH WEDGWOOD
Feb. 2nd 1805

735

Wedgwood & Bentley.

736

wedgwood WEDCWOOD

737

Wedgwood
& Bentley

738

Wedgwood & Bentley: Etruria

739

WEDGWOOD
WEDGWOOD

740

Wedgwood

741

W. & B.

742

Wedgwood
& Bentley
356

743

WEDGWOOD & SONS   WEDGWOOD

744

L. Lifsore

745

Wedgwood
& Bentley

746

Wedgwood
Wedgwood

747

WEDGWOOD

748

WEDGWOOD

146

POTTERY & PORCELAIN—ENGLAND

Date marks were introduced in 1860. They consisted of three capital letters representing month, potter, year.

Month letters 1860-1864:

J	January	Y	May	S	September
F	February	T	June	O	October
M	March	V	July	N	November
A	April	W	August	D	December

Month letters 1864-1907:

J	January	M	May	S	September
F	February	T	June	O	October
R	March	L	July	N	November
A	April	W	August	D	December

Year letters 1860-1897:

O	1860	A	1872	N	1885
P	1861	B	1873	O	1886
Q	1862	C	1874	P	1887
R	1863	D	1875	Q	1888
S	1864	E	1876	R	1889
T	1865	F	1877	S	1890
U	1866	G	1878	T	1891
V	1867	H	1879	U	1892
W	1868	I	1880	V	1893
X	1869	J	1881	W	1894
Y	1870	K	1882	X	1895
Z	1871	L	1883	Y	1896
		M	1884	Z	1897

Year letters 1898-1930:

A	1898	N	1911	A	1924
B	1899	O	1912	B	1925
C	1900	P	1913	C	1926
D	1901	Q	1914	D	1927
E	1902	R	1915	E	1928
F	1903	S	1916	F	1929
G	1904	T	1917	G	1930
H	1905	U	1918		
I	1906	V	1919		
J	1907	W	1920		
K	1908	X	1921		
L	1909	Y	1922		
M	1910	Z	1923		

GALERIE 1900

Proprietors: Barry Rose & Nicolas Polyviou

267 Camden High St, London NW1. Tel: 01-485 1001

Art Nouveau–Deco Glass, China, Metalware, Decorative Items

MON–SAT 10–5.30. SUN 11–5

A. W. Glasby & Son

Proprietor: D. E. Glasby

Leedstown, Hayle, Cornwall TR27. Tel: 0736-850303

Large Stocks of Furniture, Porcelain, Glass & Clocks.

In porcelain we try to keep a fairly large selection of figures and groups, mainly Dresden

TUESDAY TO FRIDAY 10–12.45 p.m., 2.15–5 p.m.

749  750

751

752

753

754

R Hancock, fecit

RH Worcester

755

RH

ROYAL WORCESTER

Royal Worcester Porcelain Co. 1862 onwards.

(749) Used at Worcester between 1751 and 1800

(750) Crescent with addition are rare and are usually on blue ware

(751) W is often found on a variety of patterns of early date

(752) Square marks much sought after, though they have been much copied

(753) Square marks but not so common

(754) Used on transfer prints between 1756 and 1774

(755) Used between 1756 to 1774

756
FLIGHTS

757
Flight

758

759
B

760

761

BARR FLIGHT & BARR
Royal Porcelain Works
WORCESTER
London House
No 1 Coventry Street

762
Flight Barr & Barr FBB

(756)   Sometimes impressed on the ware 1783 to 1791

(757)   Underglaze in Blue 1783 to 1791

(758)   Used on a dinner service for the Duke of Clarence

(759)   Scratched in the clay after Barr joined the firm in 1793 to about 1800

(760)   Used from 1793 to 1807

(761)   From 1807 to 1813

(762)   From 1813 to 1840

763

Chamberlains

764

Chamberlain's
Worcester
& 63, Piccadilly,
London

765

Chamberlain's
Regent China
Worcester
& 155
New Bond Street,
London.

766

767

Chamberlain's
Worcester
& 155
New Bond Street,
London

Royal Porcelain Manufacturers

768

CHAMBERLAIN & CO,
WORCESTER
155, NEW BOND STREET
& NO. 1,
COVENTRY ST
LONDON.

(763) Written with or without Worcester from from 1788 to 1808

(764) Written on specimens in 1814

(765) Printed mark used from 1800 to 1814

(766/7) Printed marks in use 1820 to 1840

(768) Printed mark used between 1840 to 1845

of London

THE FINEST
CHINA & GLASS SHOP
IN THE WORLD –
SINCE 1827

Thomas Goode & Co. Ltd.,
19 South Audley Street, Grosvenor Square,
London W1Y 6BN, England. Tel: 01-499 2823

769

Chamberlain & Co, Worcester

770

CHAMBERLAINS

771

772

773

774

775

776

(769) Printed mark used in 1847

(770) Sometimes impressed or printed, used between 1847 and 1850

(771) In use between 1850-1851

(772/3) Marks used from 1852-1862

(774) This was the trade mark of Grainger, who took over the company in 1889.

(775) John Hadley and Sons Ltd. trade mark used from 1900 to July 1905, when their business was acquired

(776) This is the general trade mark in use since 1862, it appears on all Worcester pieces

777

778

779

780

781

782

783

784

785

786

787

Anna Pottery

POTTERY & PORCELAIN
U.S.A.

(777/8) Akron China Co., Akron, Ohio.

(779) American Art Ceramic Co., Corona, N.Y. Established 1901.

(780) American Art China Works, Trenton, N.J. Established 1891.

(781/2) American China Co., Toronto, Ohio. Established 1897.

(783/4) American Crockery Co., Trenton, N.J. Established 1897.

(785/6) American Pottery Mfg. Co., Jersey City, N.J. 1833-40. *Marks printed underglaze.*

(787) Anna Pottery, Lowell, III. *Marks inscribed.*

788

789

790

791

792

793

794

795

796

797

798

(788) Beerbower, L. B. & Co., Elizabeth, N.J. From 1879. *Impressed.*

(789) Beerbower & Griffen, Phoenixville, Pa. Established 1877.

(790) Bellmark Pottery Co., Trenton, N.J. Established 1893.

(791 to 794) Bennett, Edwin, Baltimore, Md. From 1856-1890.

(795) Bennett, James, about 1840. East Liverpool, Ohio & Birmingham, Pa.

(796) Bloor, William, 1862. *Impressed.*

(797) William Brunt Pottery Co.; E. Liverpool, Ohio. 1850-1894.

(798) Buffalo Pottery about 1905, Buffalo, N.Y.

799

B-C
WILTON.

800

801

802

803

804

805

806

807

808

809

810

TEXAS

(799 to Burgess & Campbell (International
802) Pottery Co.), Trenton, N.J. Established
1860.

(803 to Burford Bros. Pottery Co., E. Liverpool,
805) Ohio. 1879-1900.

(806/7) Burroughs & Mountford, Trenton, N.J.
1879-1882.

(808/9) Carr & Morrison (New York City
Pottery), New York, N.Y. 1853-1888.

(810) Cartwright Bros., E. Liverpool, Ohio.
1880-1900.

Bell Passage Antiques

Proprietor: Mrs. D. V. Brand

36/38 High St., Wickwar, Wotton-under-Edge,
Gloucestershire GL12 8NP. Tel: 045424 251

18th & 19th CENTURY PORCELAIN, PICTURES,
GLASS & FURNITURE

Tues, Wed, Fri, Sat 9–6. *(Mon, Thurs & Sun by appointment)*

811

CHINA

812

813

814

BELLEEK

C.H.H.C.

TRADE MARK

815

CALEB CRAFTS

816

C. CROLIUS
STONEWARE MANUFACTURER
MANHATTAN WELLS
NEW-YORK

817

818

PAUL·CUSHMAN· STOE·WARE
FACTORY· 1809· HALF·A·MILE
WEST OF ALBANY GOAL

819

REX.

820

821

822

D. Dry

823

REVERE

POTTERY & PORCELAIN — U.S.A.

(811) Chelsea China Co., New Cumberland, West Vermont. Established 1888-1893. *Printed.*

(812) Chelsea Keramic Artworks, Chelsea, Mass. Established 1866.

(813) Chesapeake Pottery Co., Baltimore, Md. Established 1880. F. Haynes & Co. from 1880-1890. Haynes, Bennett & Co. from 1890.

(814) Cook Pottery Co., Trenton, N.J. Established 1894-1900.

(815) Crafts, Caleb, Portland, Me. 1837-1841. *Impressed.*

(816) Crolius, Clarkson, Sr. New York. About 1794-1837. Manhattan Wells probably not used after 1814.

(817) Crooksville China Co., Crooksville, Ohio.

(818) Crown Pottery Co., Evansville, Ind. Established 1891.

(819) Cushman, Paul. Albany N.Y. 1805-1825. *Impressed.*

(820) Dedham Pottery Co., Dedham, Mass. 1897.

(821) Derry China Co. Derry Station, Pa.

(822) Dry Bros. from about 1850.

(823) East Palestine Pottery Co. East Palestine, Ohio.

824

I.B. FARRAR & SONS

825

Fenton's Works

Bennington,
Vermont.

826

La Francaise
Porcelain

827

828

H. CANS

829

C. Gerlach

830

831

IRONSTONE CHINA
J.M. & Co.

832

833

834

D. GOODALE
HARTFORD

(824) Farrar, Isaac B. Fairfax, Vt. about 1798-1838.

(825) Fenton, C. W. Bennington, Vt. From about 1847 to 1849. *Printed.*

(826) French China Co., Sebring, Ohio.

(827) Fulper Bros. Flemington, N.J. 1805 through 19th century. *Impressed.*

(828) Gans, H. Lancaster County, Pa. about 1870.

(829) Geijsbeek Pottery Co., Golden, Colo. Established 1899.

(830) Gerlach, C. Pennsylvania. *Inscribed on redware.*

(831/2) Glasgow Pottery Co. (John Moses & Sons), Trenton, N.J. 1863-1890.

(833) Globe Pottery Co., E. Liverpool, Ohio. Established 1888. Successors to Frederick, Schenkle, Allen & Co. Established 1881.

(834) Goodale, Daniel, Hartford, Conn. 1818-1830. *Impressed.*

835

836

SETH GOODWIN

837

838

ETRUSCAN

839

840

841

843

ISAAC HEWETT
EXCELSIOR WORKS
PRICES LANDING
PENNA.

842

AH

(835) Goodwin, John, E. Liverpool, Ohio. 1844-1853. *Printed.* Succeeded by S. & W. Baggott. 1853-1895.

(836) Goodwin, Seth. Hartford, Conn. 1795-1828.

(837) Greenwood Pottery (Stephens & Tams), Trenton, N.J. Established 1861. Porcelain made after 1876. *Mark printed.*

(838) Griffen, Smith & Hill. Phoenixville, Pa. Established 1879-1890. *Impressed and* printed.

(839) Grueby Faience Co., Boston, Mass. Established 1897.

(840) Hanks & Fish, Swan Hill Pottery, South Amboy, N.J. 1849.

(841) Harker Pottery Co., E. Liverpool, Ohio. From 1890. *Marks and printed in relief.* **00** 30, Harker, Taylor & Co., existed 1847-1851. *This mark in relief.* (George S. Harker & Co. 1851-1890).

(842) Headman, Charles, Rock Hill, Pa. 1840-1870.

(843) Hewitt, Isaac, Prices Landing, Pa. 1870-1880. In blue.

844   845   846

844

6h

845

ROBLIN

846

847

Jesse Klugh

849

STONE CHINA
K. T & K.

848

WARRANTED IRON STONE CHINA
TRADE MARK
K. T. & K.

851

850

BERLIN
KT&K
CHINA

Laughlin

852

W. H. Lehew & Co
Strasburg VA

POTTERY & PORCELAIN — U.S.A.

(844) Hübener, George, Vincent, Pa. 1783-1798.

(845) Irelan Linna, San Francisco, Calif. Established 1899.

(846) Keystone Pottery Co., Trenton, N.J.

(847) Klugh, Jesse, Morgantown, Pa. 1874.

(848/9) Knowles, Taylor & Knowles, E. Liverpool, Ohio. From 1870.

(850) Knowles, Taylor & Knowles (contd).

(851) Homer Laughlin China Co., E. Liverpool, Ohio. Established 1874. *Printed.*

(852) Lehew & Co., Strasburg, Va. Established 1885. *Impressed.*

853

MADE·BY·J·LETTS

854

Johannes
Leman
❀

855

LONHUBA

856

J&J G. LOW,
PATENT
ART TILE WORKS
CHELSEA
MASS. U.S.A.
COPYRIGHT 1881 BY J&J.G. LOW

857

E Lycett

858

WARRANTED

VITREOUS GLAZE
JOHN MADDOCK & SONS
COAL PORT
TRENTON N.J.

859

POTOMAC.

J. & E. M.

860

VITREOUS
J &E. MAYER.

861

862

SEMI-GRANITE
THE D&MFR CO.
LIVERPOOL

POTTERY & PORCELAIN — U.S.A.

(853) Letts, Joshua, Cheesequake, N.J. 1810-1815.

(854) Leman, Johannes, Tyler's Port, Pa. c.1830.

(855) Lonhuda Pottery, Steubenville, Ohio. Established 1892.

(856) Low Art Tile Co., Chelsea, Mass. Established 1887-1888.

(857) Lycett, Edward, Atlanta, Ga. Established 1890.

(858) John Maddock & Sons, Trenton, N.J. From 1894.

(859/ 860) Mayer Pottery Co., Beaver Falls, Pa. Established 1881.

(861) McLaughlin, M. L. Cincinnati, Ohio. Established 1876.

(862) D. E. McNicol Pottery Co., E. Liverpool, Ohio. From 1892.

863

IRONSTONE CHINA
MERCER POTTERY CO

864

865

866

867

868

IRONSTONE CHINA
O. P. Co

869

Samuel Paul

870

MADE by XERXES
PRICE S. AMBOY

871

D__D

872

873

(863) Mercer Pottery Co., Trenton, N.J. Established 1868-1869.

(864) Merrimac Ceramic Co., Newburyport, Mass. Established 1897.

(865) Monmouth Pottery Co., Monmouth, Ill. About 1890.

(866) New England Pottery Co., Boston, Mass. Established 1875-1887.

(867) Ohio China Co., E. Palestine, Ohio.

(868) Onondaga Pottery Co., Syracuse, N.Y. Established 1871.

(869) Paul, Samuel, Pennsylvania.

(870) Price, Xerxes, Sayreville, N.J. About 1802. *Impressed.*

(871) Prospect Hill Pottery Co., Trenton, N.J. Established 1880.

(872) Rookwood Pottery, Cincinnati, Ohio. Established 1879.

(873) Rouse & Turner, Jersey City, N.J. Established 1859-1892.

874

Salamander Works Woodbridge N. J

875

876

Charles Laubach 1810 Patern Durham Pa Made at Singer's Pottery Haycock

877

I. Smith.

878

made by Henry Stockwell

POTTERY & PORCELAIN — U.S.A.

(874)   Salamander Works, Woodbridge, **N.J.** Established 1825-1896. *Impressed*.

(875)   School, Michael, Tylersport, Montgomery Co. Pa. About 1830. *Impressed*.

(876)   Singer, Simon, Haycock, Pa. c.1810.

(877)   Smith, Joseph, Wrightstown, Pa. 1763 to about 1800.

(878)   Stockwell, Henry, Colombian **Factory,** Perth Amboy, **N.J.** 1831.

June Spinella Porcelain Restorers

Proprietor: June Spinella

The Studio, Igastein Rd, London W6, England
Tel: 01-385 7512

Certain amount of porcelain and small picture gallery
Ceramic conservation and courses in ceramic restoration
MONDAY–FRIDAY 9.30–6.00

879

C. TUPPER
PORTAGE CO.
O.

880

881

 SIGSBEE

882

883

HOTEL

884

Cosian
WELLER

885

P P W C

886

AVON
W R₁
CO

887

B X B

888

(879) Tupper, C., Portage County, Ohio. c.1870. *Impressed.*

(880) Union Potteries Co., E. Liverpool, Ohio. Late 19th century.

(881) Vickers, T. & J. Caln & Lionville, Pa. From 1806.

(882) Vodrey Bros., E. Liverpool, Ohio. 1857-1885.

(883) Warwick China Co., Wheeling, W. Va. Established 1887.

(884) Weller, S. A., Zanesville, Ohio. Late 19th century.

(885) Wellsville China Co., Wellsville, Ohio. Established 1879.

(886) Wheeling Potteries Co., Wheeling, W. Va. Established 1903.

(887) Wheeling Pottery Co., Wheeling, W. Va. Established 1879.

(888) Willetts Mfg. Co., Trenton, N.J. Established 1879.

889 洪武年製

890 永樂年製

891 大明宣德年製

892 大明成化年製

893 大明弘治年製

894 大明正德年製

895 大明嘉靖年製

896 大明隆慶年製

897 大明萬曆年製

898 大明天啟年製

899 崇禎年製

CHINESE REIGN MARKS

Marks are painted in blue on porcelain, on the base of the piece. There are European imitations of the marks.

Ming Dynasty Marks 1368-1643

(889)	Hung Wu 1368-1398
(890)	Yung Lo 1403-1424
(891)	Hsüan Tê 1426-1435
(892)	Ch'êng Hua 1465-1487
(893)	Hung Chih 1488-1505
(894)	Chêng Tê 1506-1521
(895)	Chia Ching 1522-1566
(896)	Lung Ch'ing 1567-1572
(897)	Wan Li 1573-1619
(898)	T'ien Ch'i 1621-1627
(899)	Ch'ung Chêng 1628-1643

Ch'ing Dynasty Marks 1644-1909

(900)	Shun Chih 1644-1661
(901)	K'ang Hsi 1662-1722
(902)	Yung Chêng 1723-1735
(903)	Ch'ien Lung 1736-1795
(904)	Chia Ch'ing 1796-1820
(905)	Tao Kuang 1821-1850
(906)	Hsien Fêng 1851-1861
(907)	T'ung Chih 1862-1874
(908)	Kuang Hsü 1875-1909

CHINESE REIGN MARKS

900
大清雍正年製

901
大清康熙年製

902
大清順治年製

903
大清乾隆年製

904
嘉慶年製

905
大清道光年製

906
大清咸豐年製

907
大清同治年製

908
大清光緒年製

JAPANESE DATE MARKS

Japanese marks on ceramics are stamped, painted, or incised on the wares. They can be written in Chinese characters. Japanese potters did not sign their work before 19th century.

德建	Ken-tok 1370		正文	Bun-show 1466
中文	Bun-tin 1372		仁廏	O-nin 1467
授天	Ten-du 1375		明文	Bun-mei 1469
和弘	Ko-wa 1380		亨長	Chiyo-kiyo 1487
中元	Gen-tin 1380		德延	En-tok 1489
四德明	Mei-tok 1393		應明	Mei-o 1492
永廏	O-yei 1394		龜文	Bun-ki 1501
長正	Show-tiyo 1428		正水	Yei-show 1504
享永	Yei-kiyo 1429		永大	Dai-jei 1521
吉嘉	Ka-kitsu 1441		祓亨	Kiyo-rok 1528
安文	Bun-an 1444		永大	Di-yei 1532
德宝	Ho-tok 1449		治弘	Ko-dsi 1555
德亨	Kiyo-tok 1452		祿永	Yei-rok 1558
正康	Ko-show 1455		龜兄	Gen-ki 1570
祿長	Chiyo-rok 1457		正天	Ten-show 1573
正寬	Kwan-show 1460		祿文	Bun-rok 1592

JAPANESE DATE MARKS

長慶	Kei-chiyo 1596	享延	Yen-kiyo 1744
和元	Gen-wa 1615	延寛	Kwan-jen 1748
永寛	Kwan-jei 1624	暦寳	Ho-reki 1751
保正	Show-ho 1644	和明	Mei-wa 1764
安慶	Kei-an 1648	永安	An-jei 1772
應承	Show-o 1652	明天	Ten-mei 1781
暦明	Mei-reki 1655	政寛	Kwan-sei 1789
治萬	Man-dsi 1658	和享	Kiyo-wa 1801
文寛	Kwan-bun 1661	化文	Bun-kwa 1804
寳延	Yen-po 1673	政文	Bun-sei 1818
和天	Ten-wa 1681	保天	Ten-po 1834
享貞	Tei-kiyo 1684	化弘	Ko-kua 1844
祿元	Gen-rok 1688	永嘉	Ka-yei 1848
永寳	Ho-yei 1704	久文	Bun-se 1854
德正	Show-tok 1711	治元	Man-yen 1860
保享	Kiyo-ho 1717	應慶	Bun-kin 1861
文元	Gen-bun 1736	治明	Gen-di 1861
保寛	Kwan-po 1741	政安	Kei-o 1865

Mei-di 1868

延萬